REAL WORLD MATH FOR THINKING KIDS

Data Hunt

Gathering and Using Data to Communicate About Ourselves

Published in cooperation with
American Bar Association
Special Committee on Youth Education for Citizenship
Chicago, Illinois

Published by Scholastic Inc. Printed in U.S.A.
ISBN 0-590-27886-X
1 2 3 4 5 6 7 8 9 10 09 01 00 99 98 97 96 95 94

We collect, organize, represent, and use information to draw conclusions about our world.

Data Hunt

We sort, display, and interpret data to learn more about ourselves.

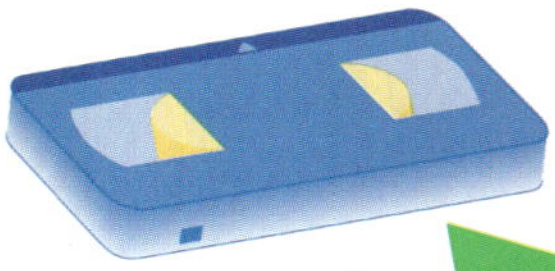

Video

SUBCONCEPT 1

We count and sort objects according to their attributes.

Read Aloud

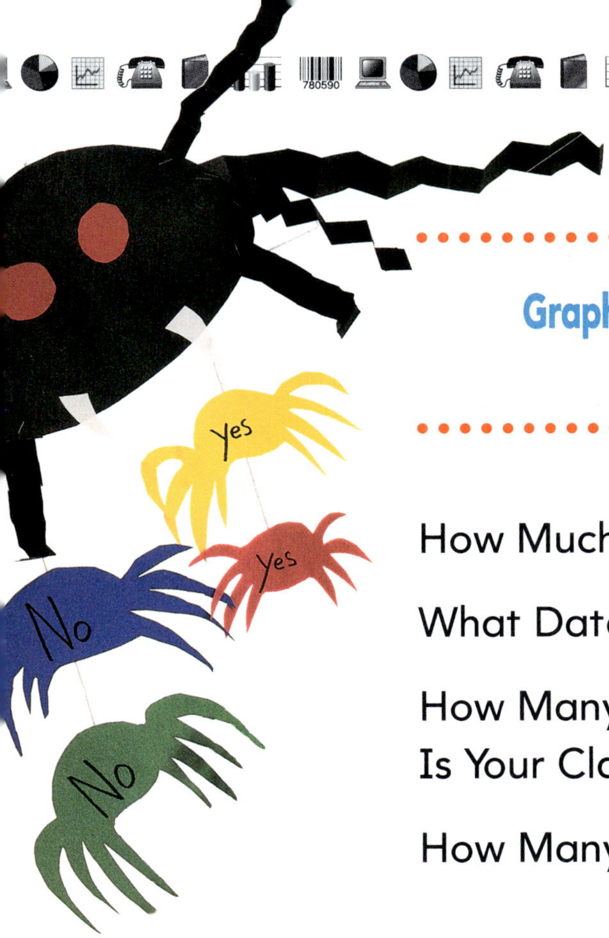

SUBCONCEPT 2

Graphs help us visually compare data and provide information we can add and subtract.

SUBCONCEPT 3

We display data in different ways in order to make it easy to interpret and compute.

Big Book

What Will Go in Your Class Data Book?

What do you find in books? Some books give us information. Information told with numbers is often called data. What data could you put in a book about your class?

Plan a class data book.

DO·IT

- Start a list of things that tell about your class.
- What do you like to do? What other things can you think of that tell about you?

SHARE·IT

- How can you show the information in a book?

BUILD·ON·IT

- Start a class data book.
- Make a cover for the book. How can you show everyone in the class on the cover?

THINK

What does everyone in your class have in common?

Where Does Your Shoe Fit?

There are many things to discover about you and your classmates. Work from your feet up. Look at your shoes!

You can use:
- Paper
- Pencil
- Shoes

Sort your shoes.

DO·IT
- Think of ways to sort the shoes in your class. Then sort them.
- Where does your shoe fit when the class sorts its shoes?

SHARE·IT
- How can you and your classmates keep a record of your sorting?

BUILD·ON·IT
- Write what you learned about your shoes. Put what you learned into your class data book.

THINK

Why are there so many kinds of shoes?

What Else Can You See and Sort?

You have sorted your shoes. Now take a look at your tops. What can you tell about these children's tops?

Sort your tops.

DO·IT

- Work with a group.
- Each of you make a drawing to show your top.
- Sort the drawings.

SHARE-IT

- Tell how your group sorted its tops.
- In what other ways can you sort your tops?

BUILD-ON-IT

- Pick other things you can describe and sort. Start sorting.
- Draw pictures to show how you sorted.

THINK

How many ways can you sort the names in your class?

What Will Your Flag Look Like?

What are your favorite colors? You can use them to make a flag.

Papua New Guinea

Chad

Ethiopia

Spain

Panama

You can use:

- Construction paper
- Crayons or markers

Indonesia

Design a flag.

DO·IT

- Use your favorite colors to make a flag.
- How many parts will your flag have?

SHARE·IT

- Share your flags.
- How are all of your flags alike? How are they different?

BUILD·ON·IT

- Sort the flags your class made. What is the most popular color? design?

THINK

How is the flag of the United States divided?

What Is Your Favorite Food?

Just about everyone has a favorite food. What is yours? How many other children in your class like the same food?

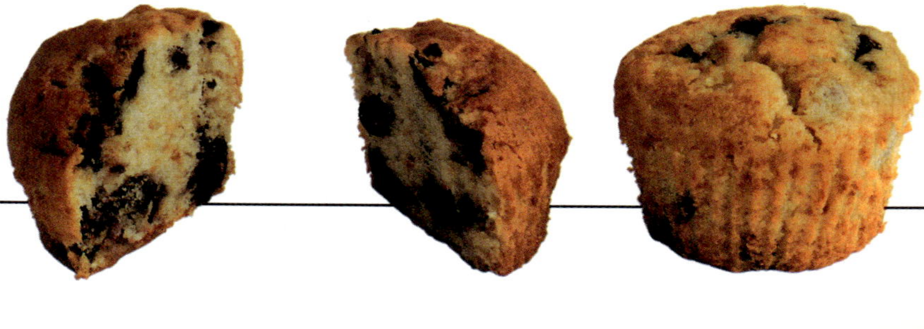

Sort favorite foods.

DO-IT
- Work with other students in your class. Draw pictures of your favorite foods.
- Sort the pictures.
- Label how you sorted them.

SHARE-IT
- Talk about the favorite foods in your class.
- How else could you sort them?

BUILD-ON-IT
- Put something you have learned about favorite foods in the class data book.

THINK

If you could serve three kinds of food at a class party, what would they be? Why?

What Do You Like Best?

Think of one thing you like best. It could be an animal. It could be a sport. It could be something you play with.

Compare favorites.

DO·IT

- Make a drawing of your favorite thing. Stand with classmates who like the same kind of thing you do.

SHARE·IT

- How many children are in each group?
- Which group is the largest? Which one is the smallest?

BUILD·ON·IT

- Sort the favorite things in your group in different ways.
- Put what you have learned in the class data book.

How Much Can Your Hand Hold?

How many counters can you hold in your hand? Estimate.

Grab some counters.

You can use:
- Counters
- Construction paper
- Markers or crayons

DO·IT
- Grab some counters. Estimate, and then count them.
- Make a record of how many you grabbed.
- Get together with other students who grabbed as many counters as you.

SHARE·IT
- How many students are in each group?

BUILD·ON·IT
- How can the class display its data? Do it.
- Add the data to your class data book.

THINK

What else could you do to show how much your hand can hold?

What Data Can You Find?

Look closely at the graph.
What does it tell you?

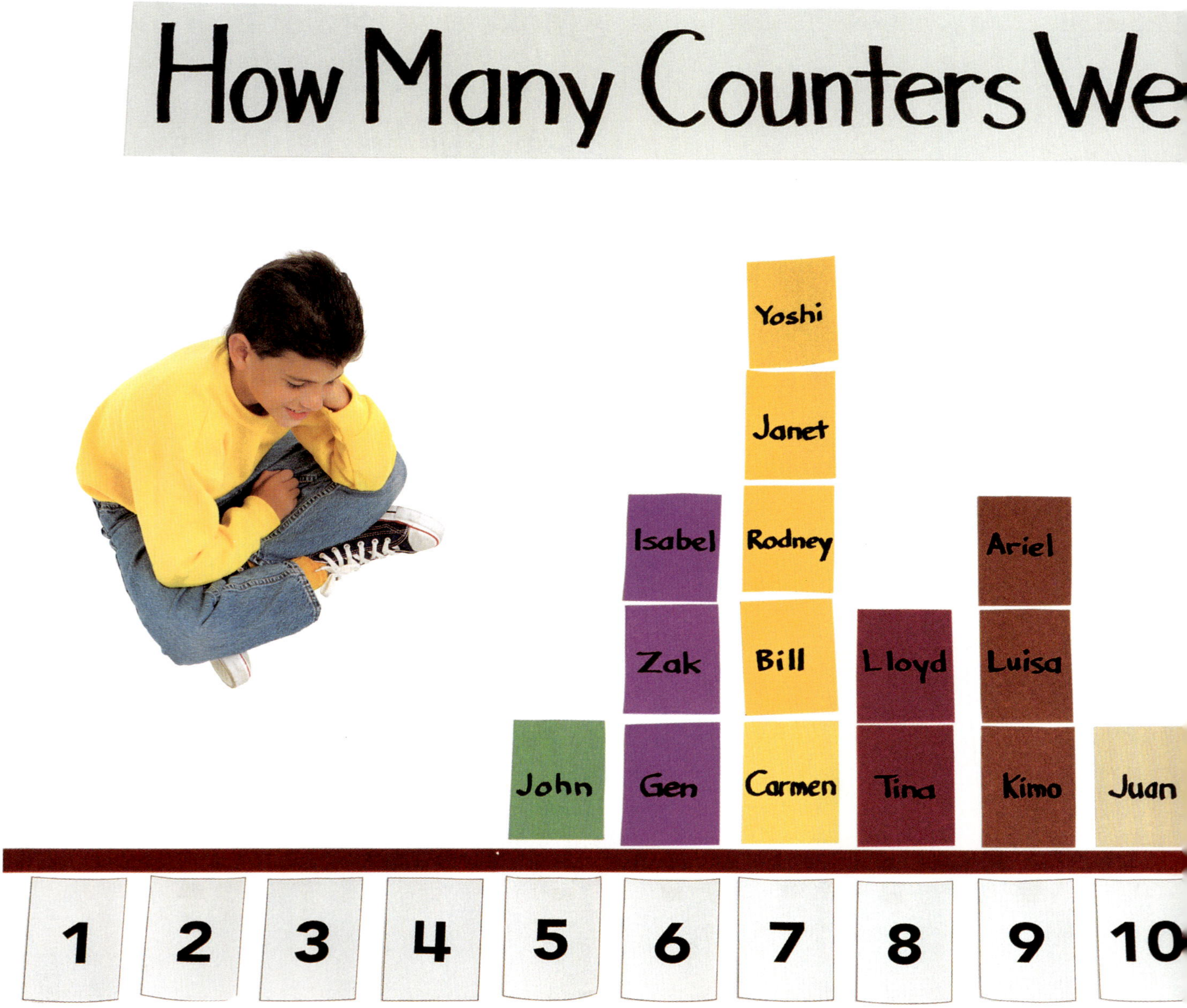

You can use:

- Paper
- Pencil
- Calculator

Interpret data.

DO·IT

- Look at the graph. How many kids grabbed 10 counters? How many grabbed 7? How many grabbed 15?

SHARE·IT

- Tell what other data you can find on the graph.

BUILD·ON·IT

- Look at how your class showed its data when you grabbed the counters. How is it like this graph? How is it different?
- Did your class grab about as many counters as these children?

THINK

How can a calculator help you interpret data?

How Many Giant Steps Long Is Your Classroom?

How long is your giant step? How many steps would it take for you to go from one end of the classroom to the other? Estimate.

Take a giant step.

DO·iT

- Take giant steps across your classroom.
- Have a partner count your steps.

SHARE·iT

- Work with the whole class. Make a graph to show how many giant steps each of you took.
- What was the most common number of steps the class took?

BUILD·ON·iT

- Write a number story about your class's giant steps.

You can use:

- Paper
- Pencil
- Graph paper

THINK

Where on your graph would your teacher's steps go?

How Many Hops Can You Hop in One Minute?

Beat the clock! See how many times you can hop in a given time.

Get hopping.

You can use:
- Stopwatch
- Construction paper
- Pencil

DO·IT

- Predict how many times you can hop in 1 minute. Now hop to it!
- How many hops did you hop?

SHARE·IT

- Make a graph to show how many times each of you hopped.

BUILD·ON·IT

- What are the most hops anyone hopped? What is the least?
- Put the information in your class data book.

THINK

Does the graph tell how high people hopped?

How Else Can You Show Data?

What questions do you think these girls are asking? What are the possible answers to these questions?

Take a survey.

DO·IT

- Think of a question that can be answered yes or no.
- Ask other students your question.
- Find a way to show how your classmates answered.

SHARE·IT

- Tell what you learned about your class.

BUILD·ON·IT

- What other questions can you ask? Find ways to show how the class answered them.

You can use:

- Hangers
- Construction paper
- Scissors
- Markers
- Tape

THINK

How is "do you like spiders?" different from the question "What do you like?"

What Data Are in Your Mouth?

What can you say about these children's teeth? What can you guess about Mei's teeth?

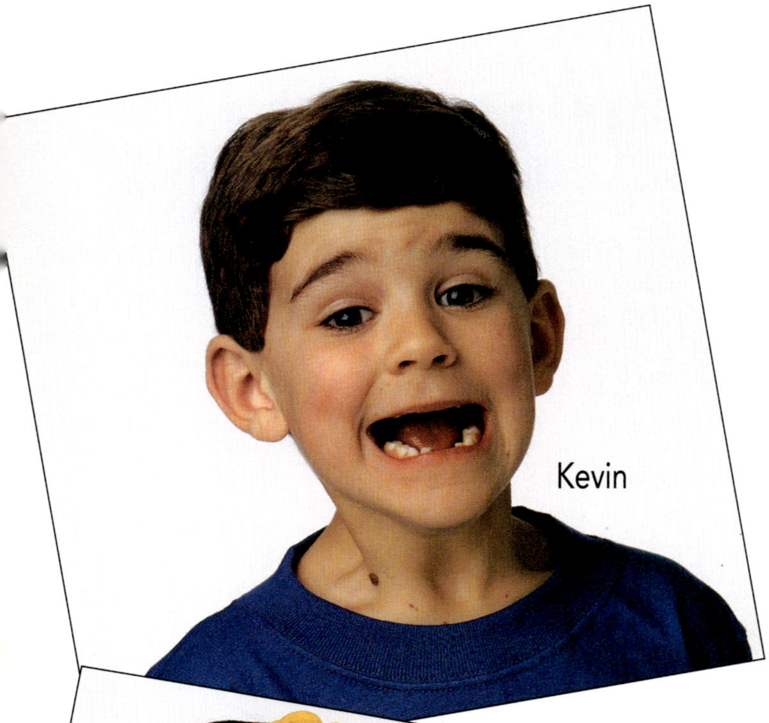

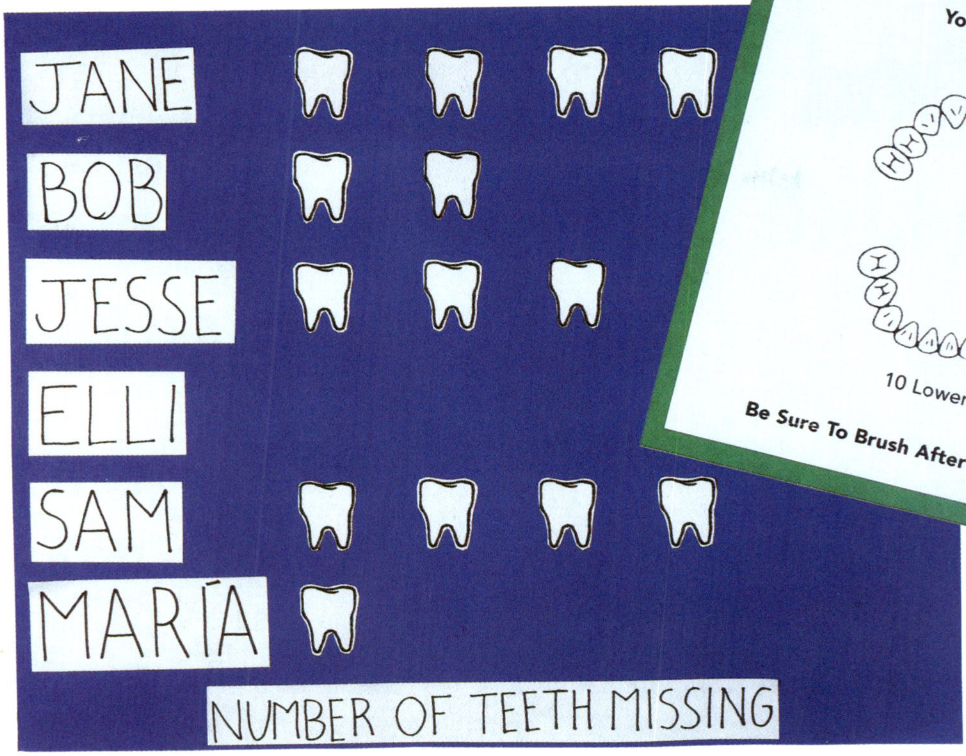

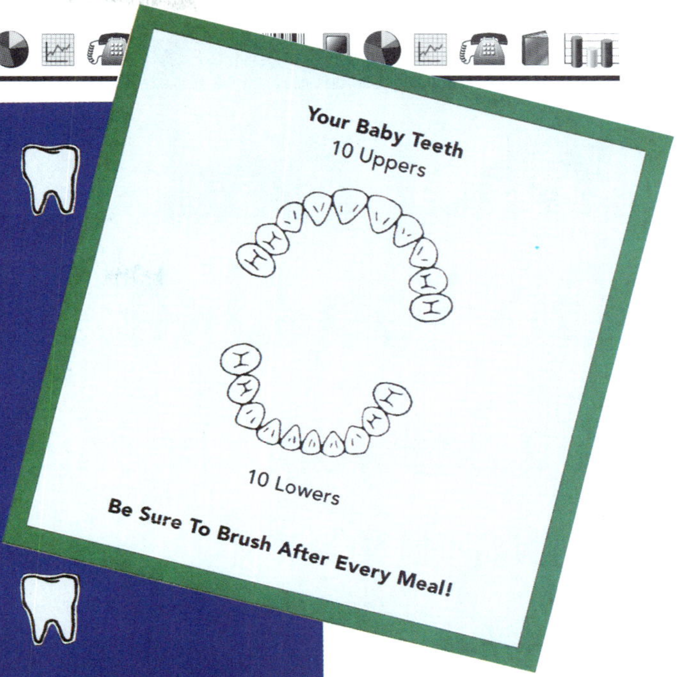

Count your teeth.

DO·IT

- Work with the whole class.
- Find the number of teeth each of you is missing. Find the class total.

SHARE·IT

- Make a graph to show the data your class found.

BUILD·ON·IT

- Put the total number of missing teeth in your class data book.
- Write a number story about your class's missing teeth.

THINK

How can you tell the number of teeth you have without counting them all?

What Kind of Books Do You Like Best?

You and your classmates read many books. What is your favorite kind?

Graph your books.

You can use:
Book cards
Markers or crayons

DO·IT • How can you and your classmates sort your favorite books? What categories can you use?

SHARE·IT • Make a graph to show the favorite kinds of books in your class.

BUILD·ON·IT • What is the most popular kind of book in your class? What else can you add to your class data book?

THINK

If you read 1 book a day, how many will you read in 1 week? 2 weeks?

What Happens in Your Day?

How do you and your classmates keep busy? Think of what you do every day. What do you like doing best?

Show your schedule.

DO·IT

- Work with the class. List what you do every day.
- Each of you draw a picture of your favorite thing on the list.
- Put the pictures in order.

You can use:
Paper
Pencil
Picture of your favorite thing

SHARE·IT

- What is the most popular thing the class does?

BUILD·ON·IT

- Work with a partner.
- Show how you spend your Saturdays. Make a schedule.

THINK

What do you do once a year?

What Can You Say About Yourself?

What have you learned about yourself? Make a poster about you. You can get ideas from your class data book.